I0841179

Vol 10

MAZE

Ages 4-6

FOR KIDS

MAZE BOOK

SOCIAL MEDIA

Ⓕ /MySweetBooks1

Ⓣ /MySweetBooks1

Ⓘ /MySweetBooks1

Ⓟ /MySweetBooks

Email Us : mysweetbooks1@gmail.com

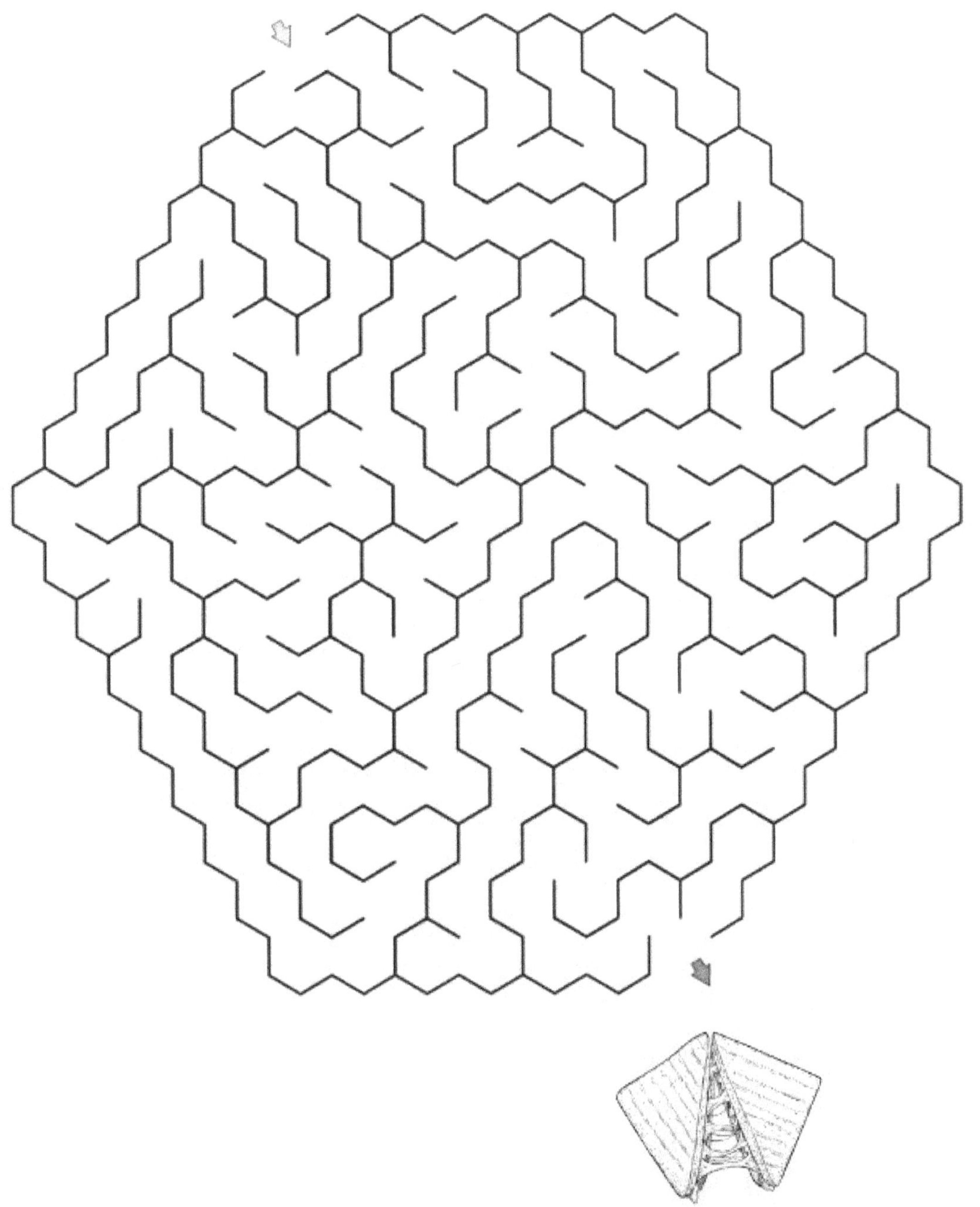

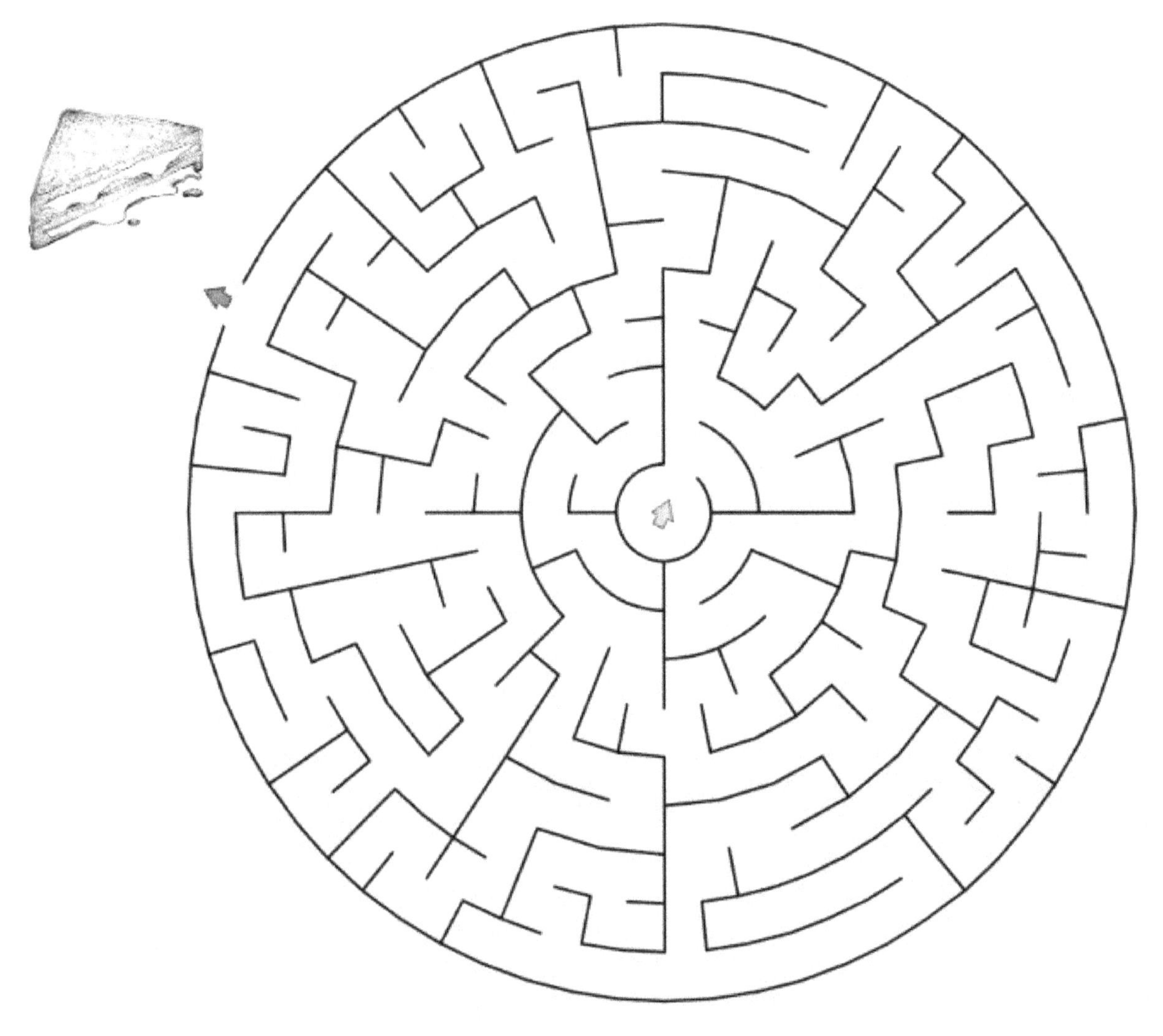

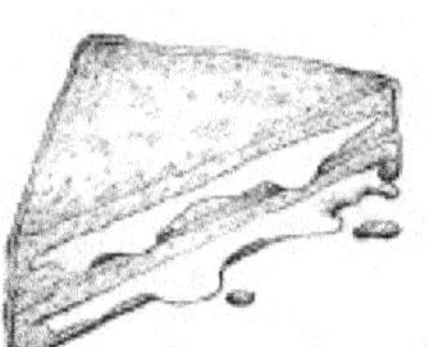

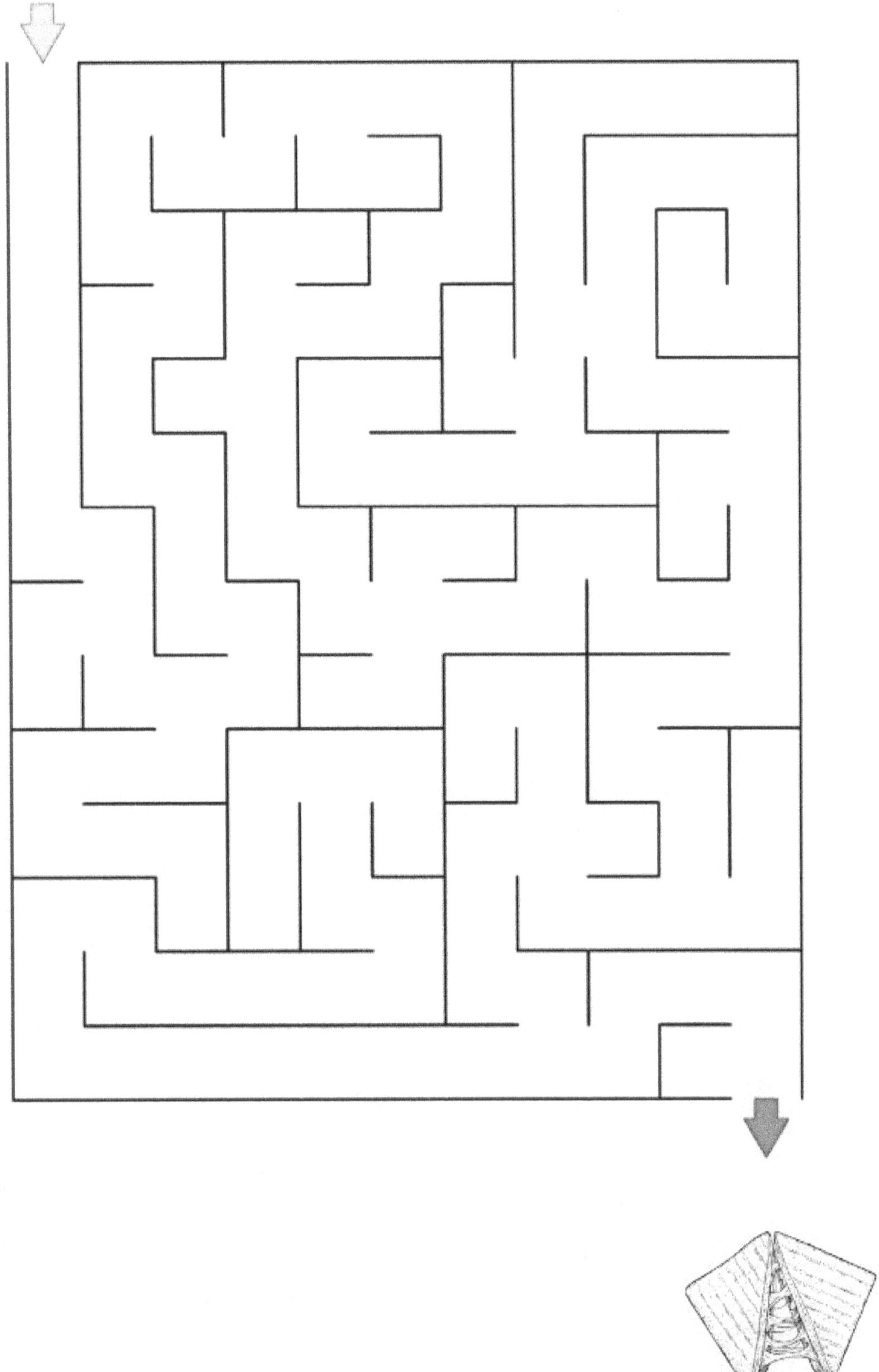

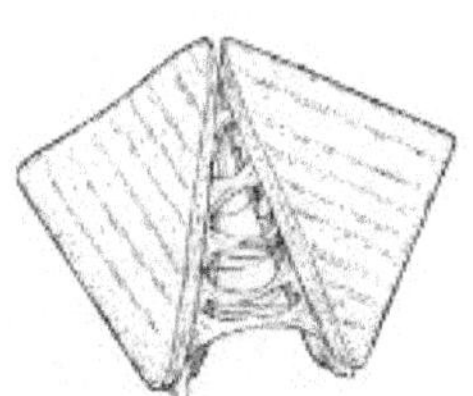

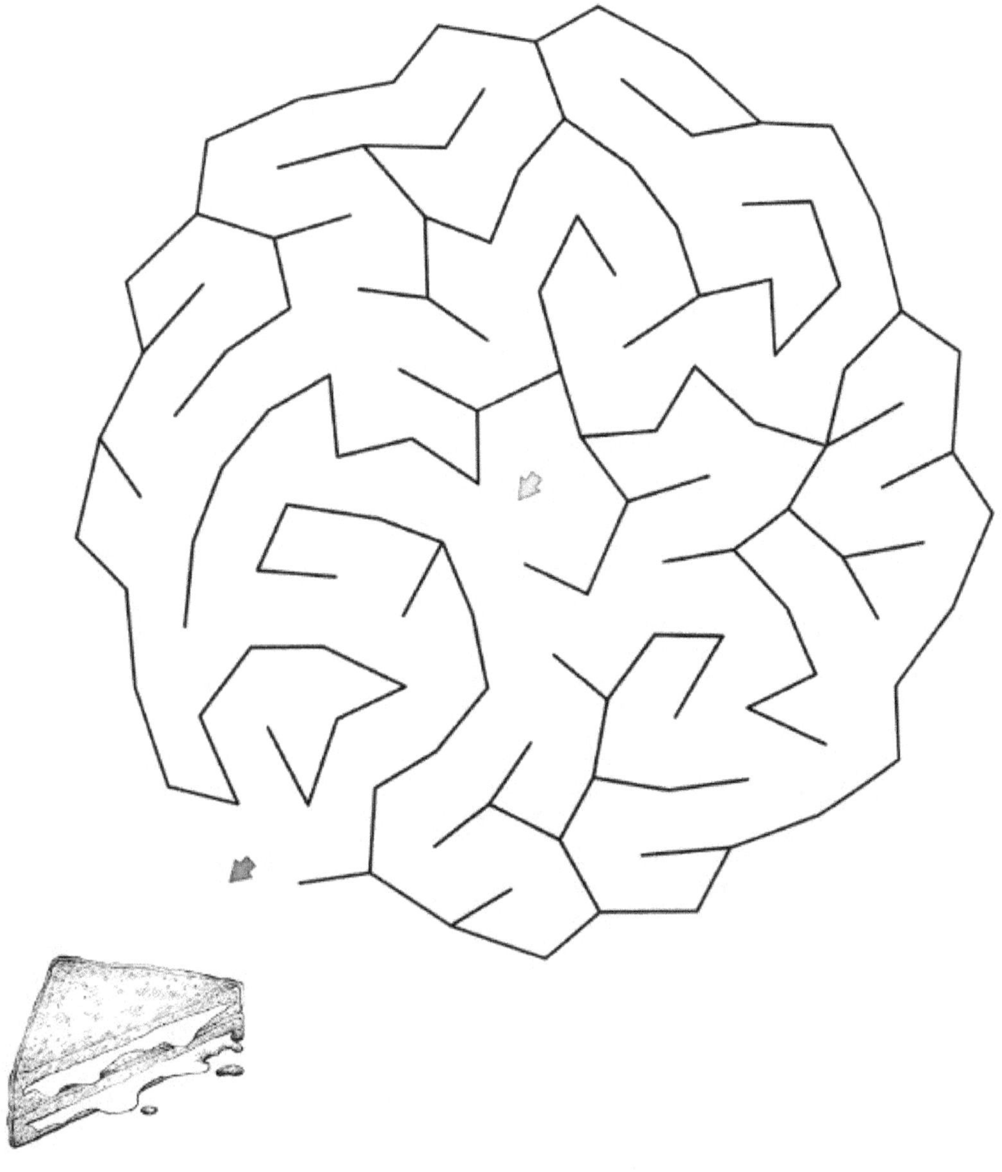

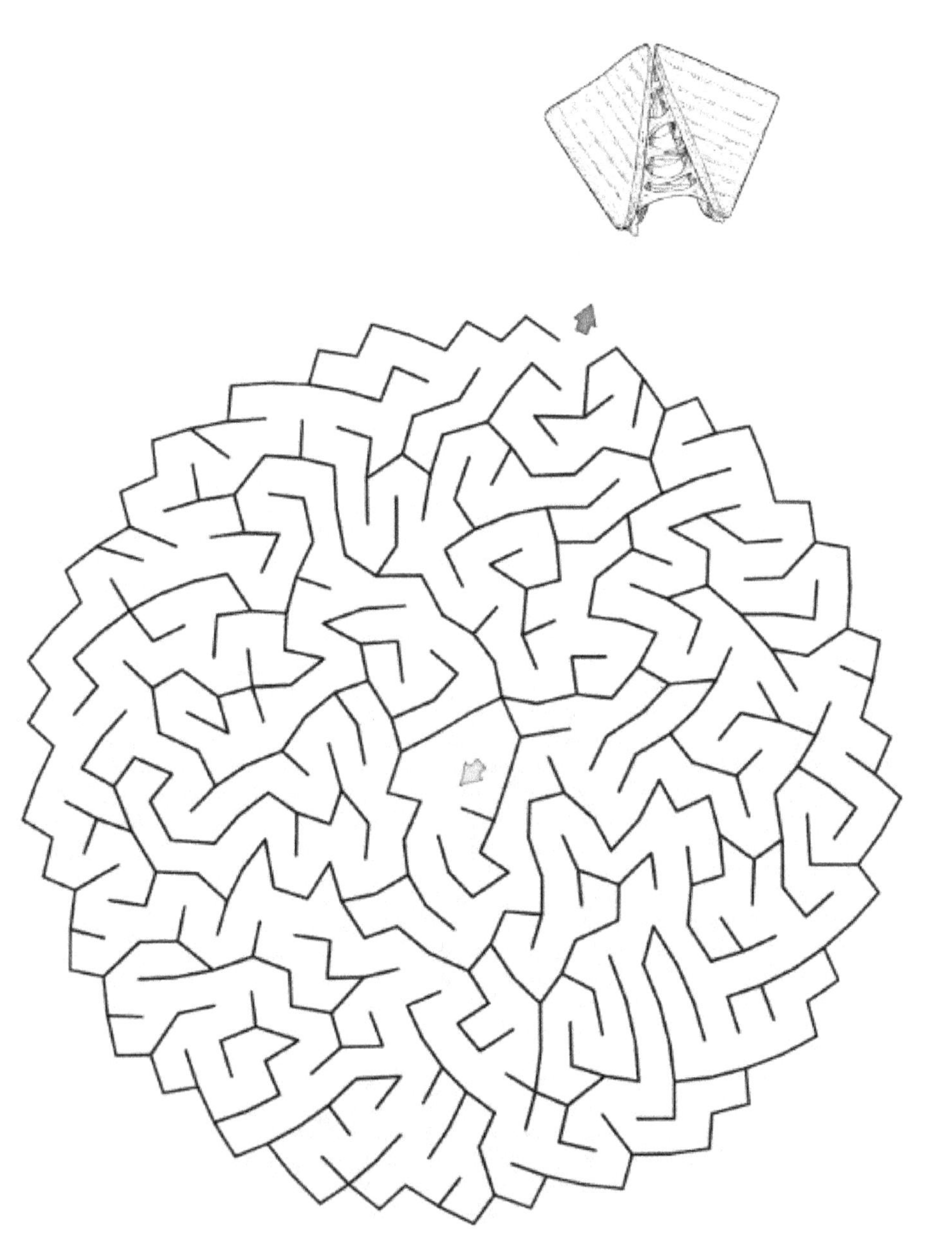

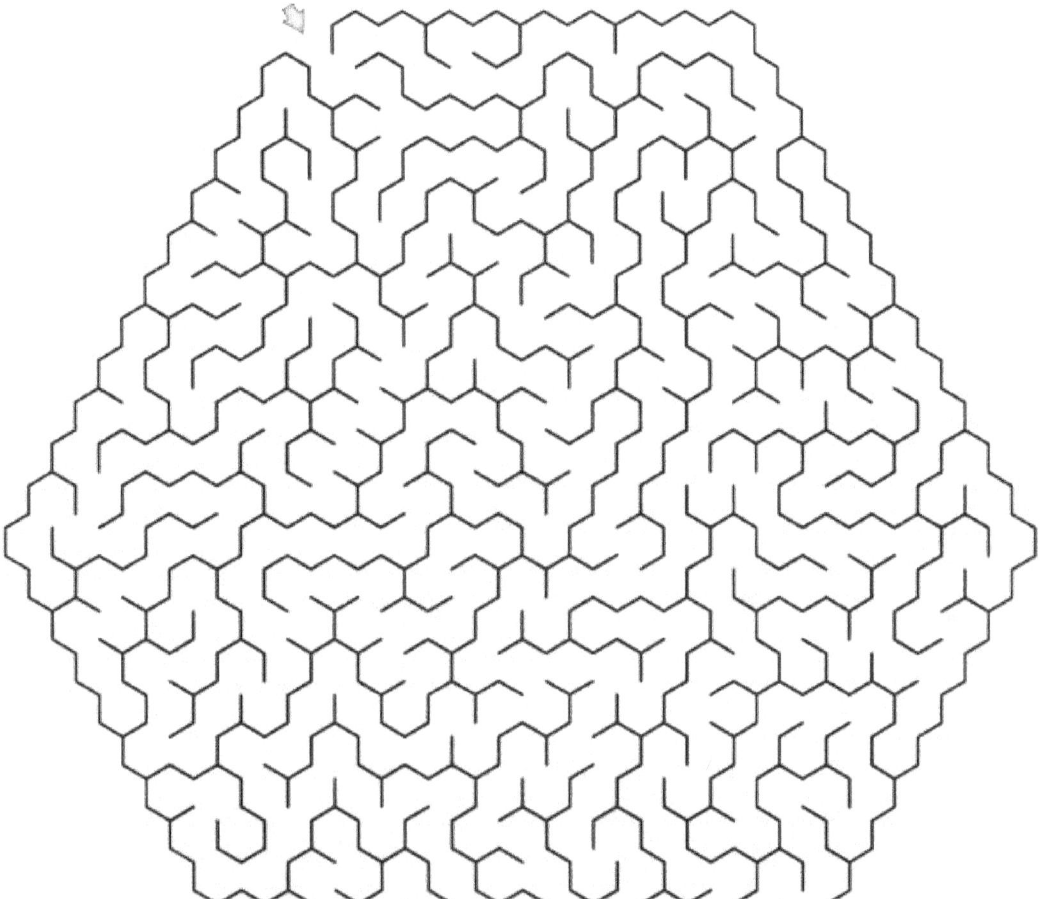

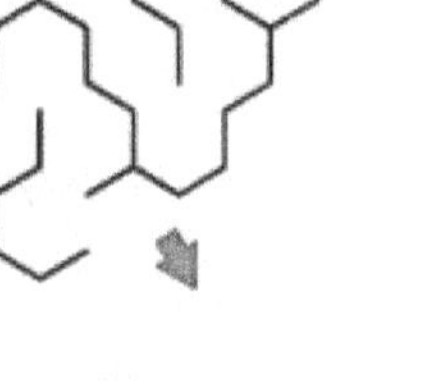

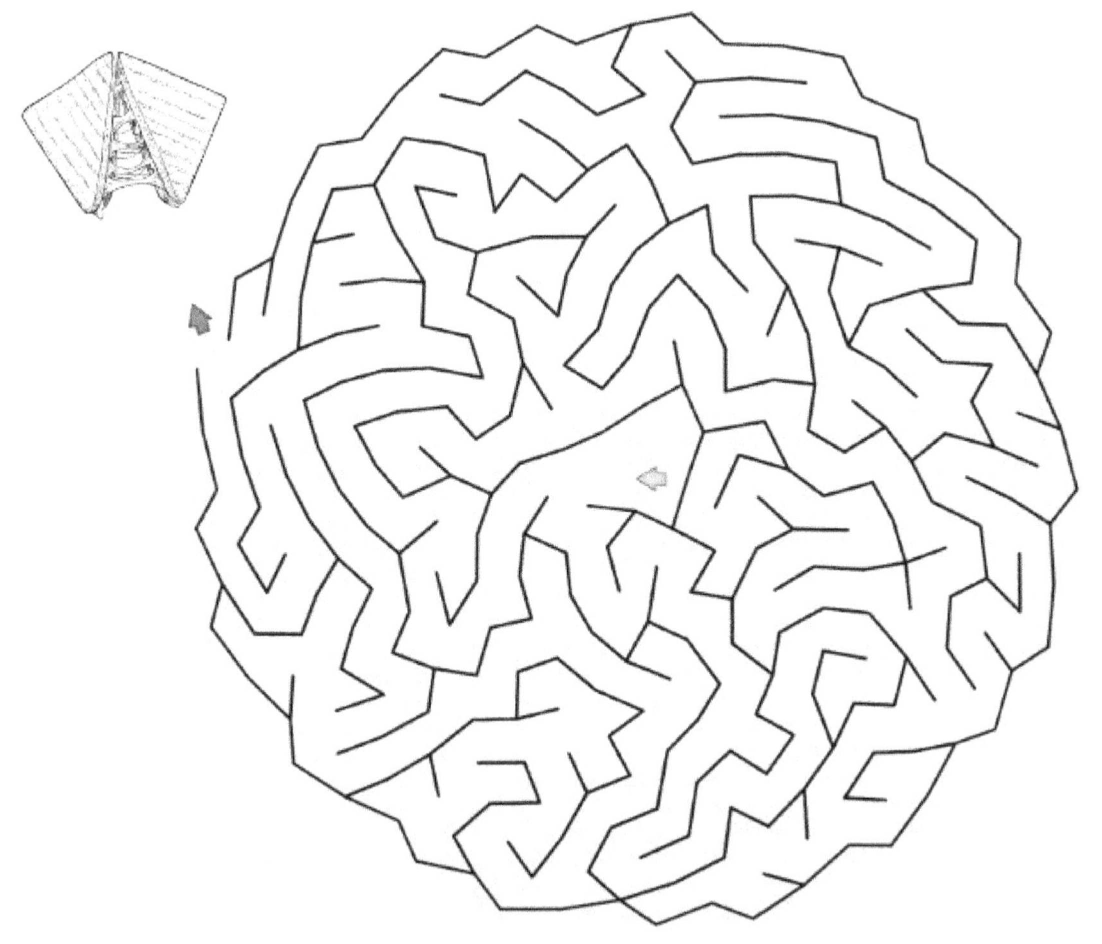

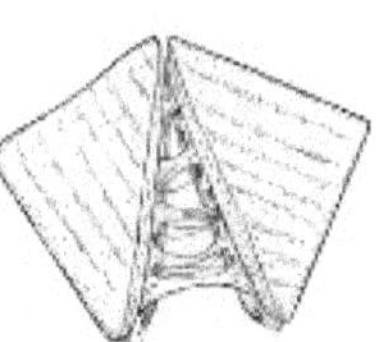

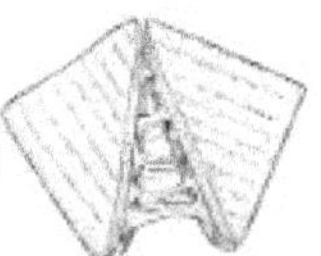

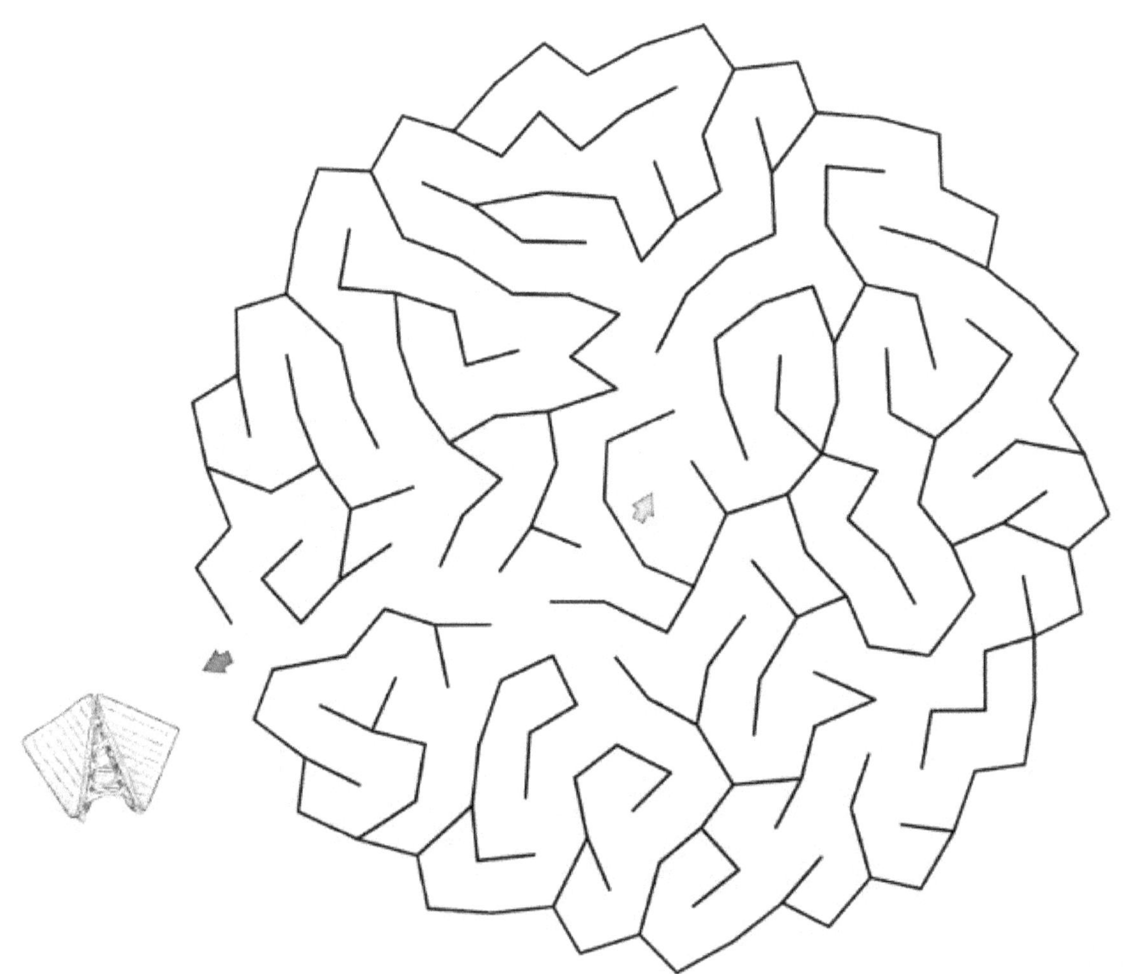

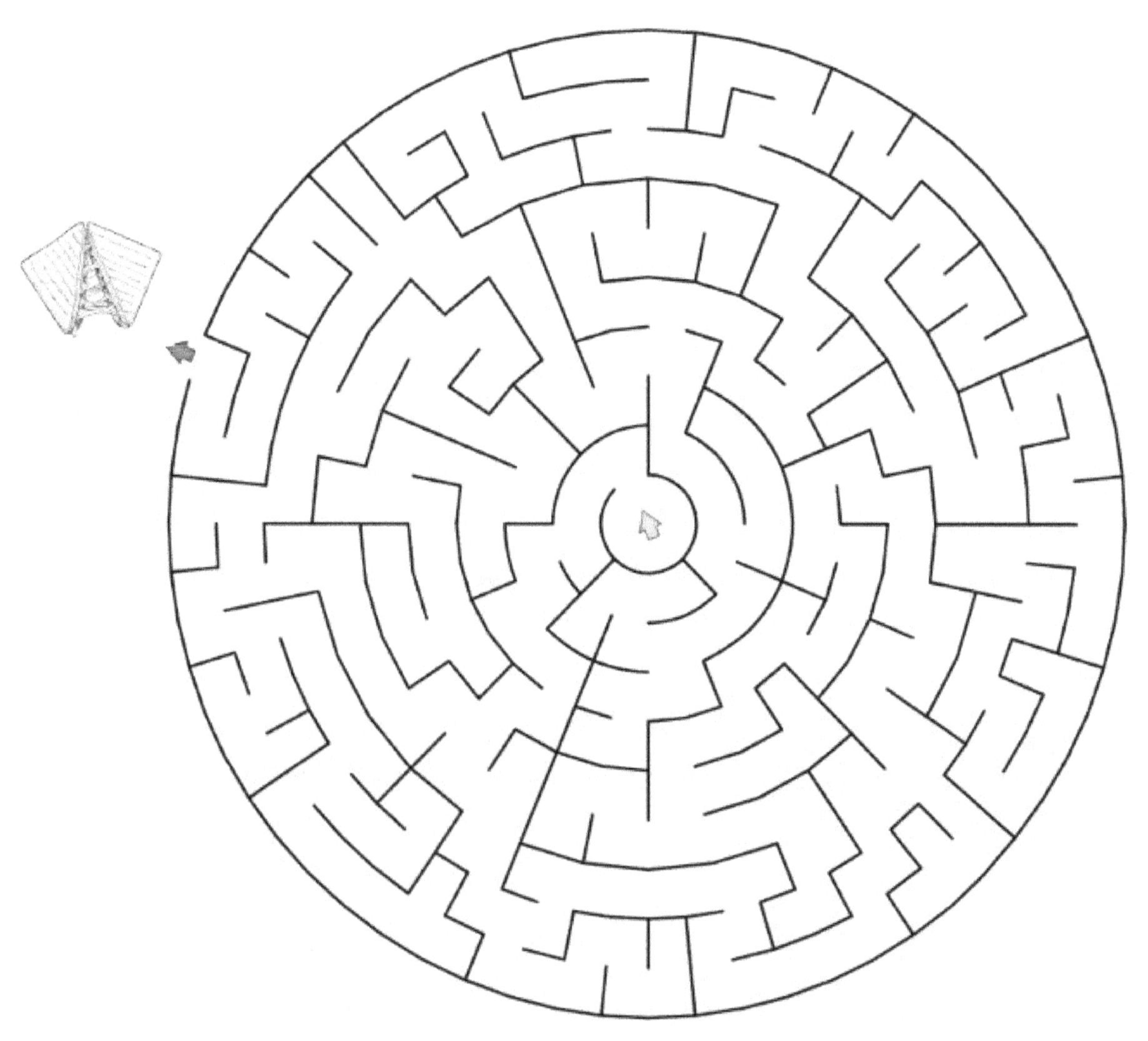

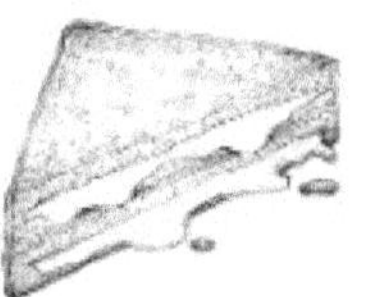

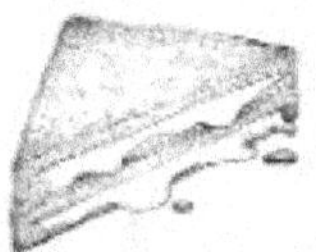

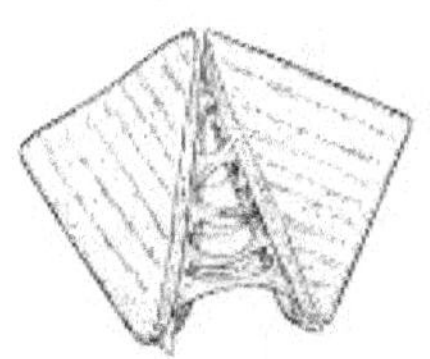

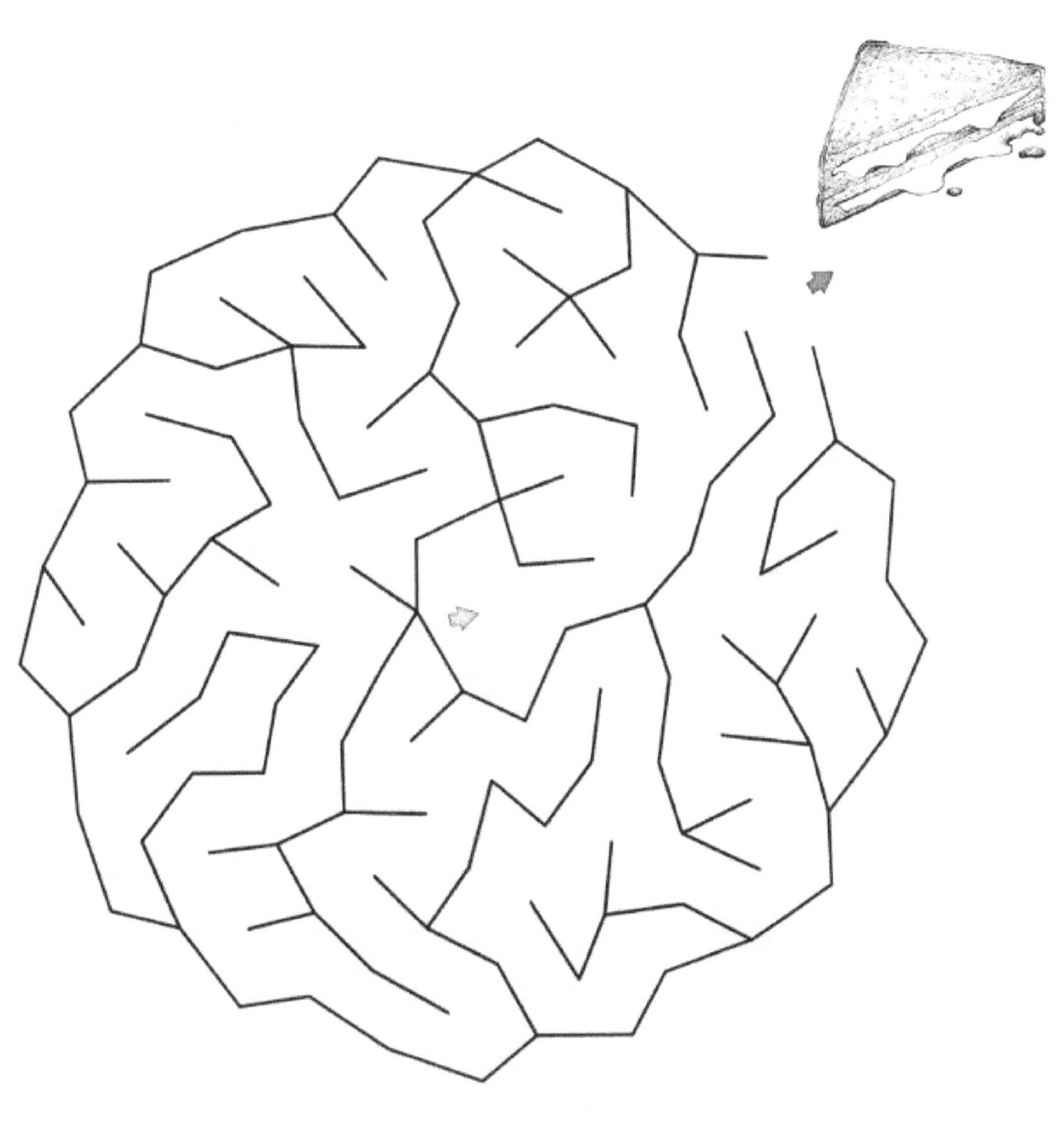

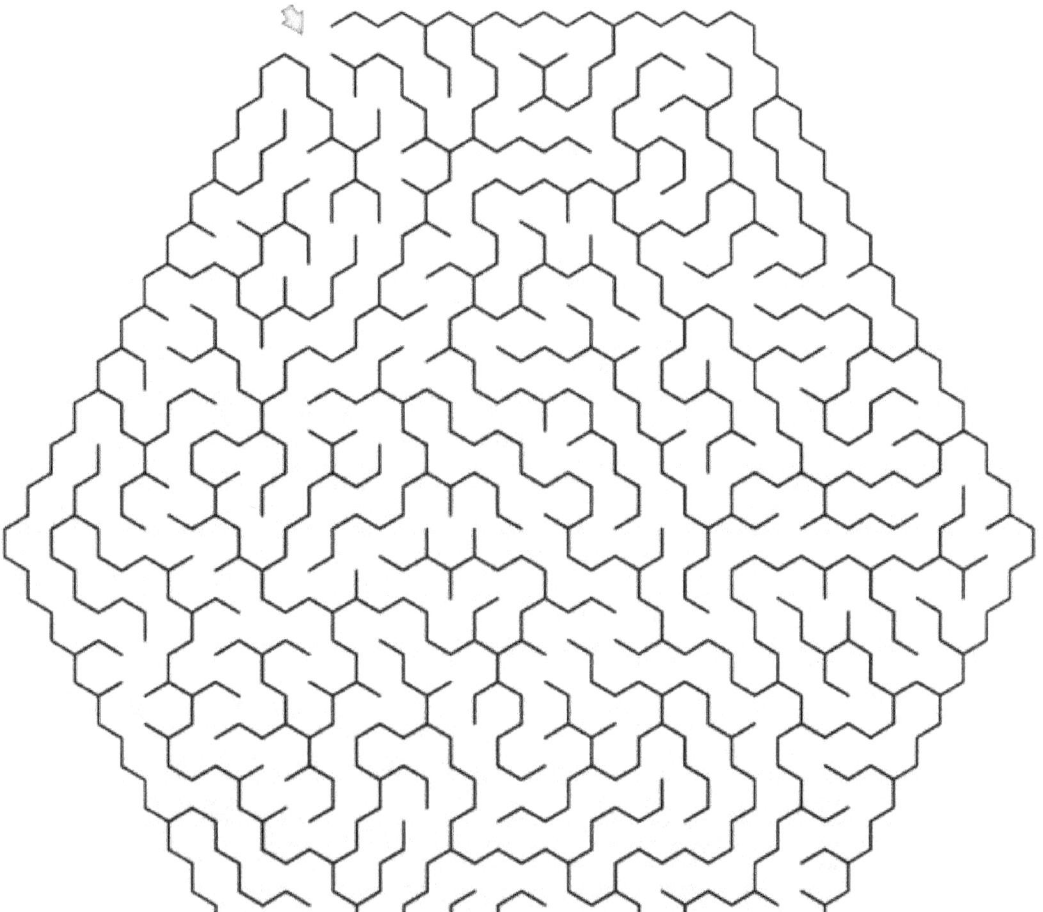

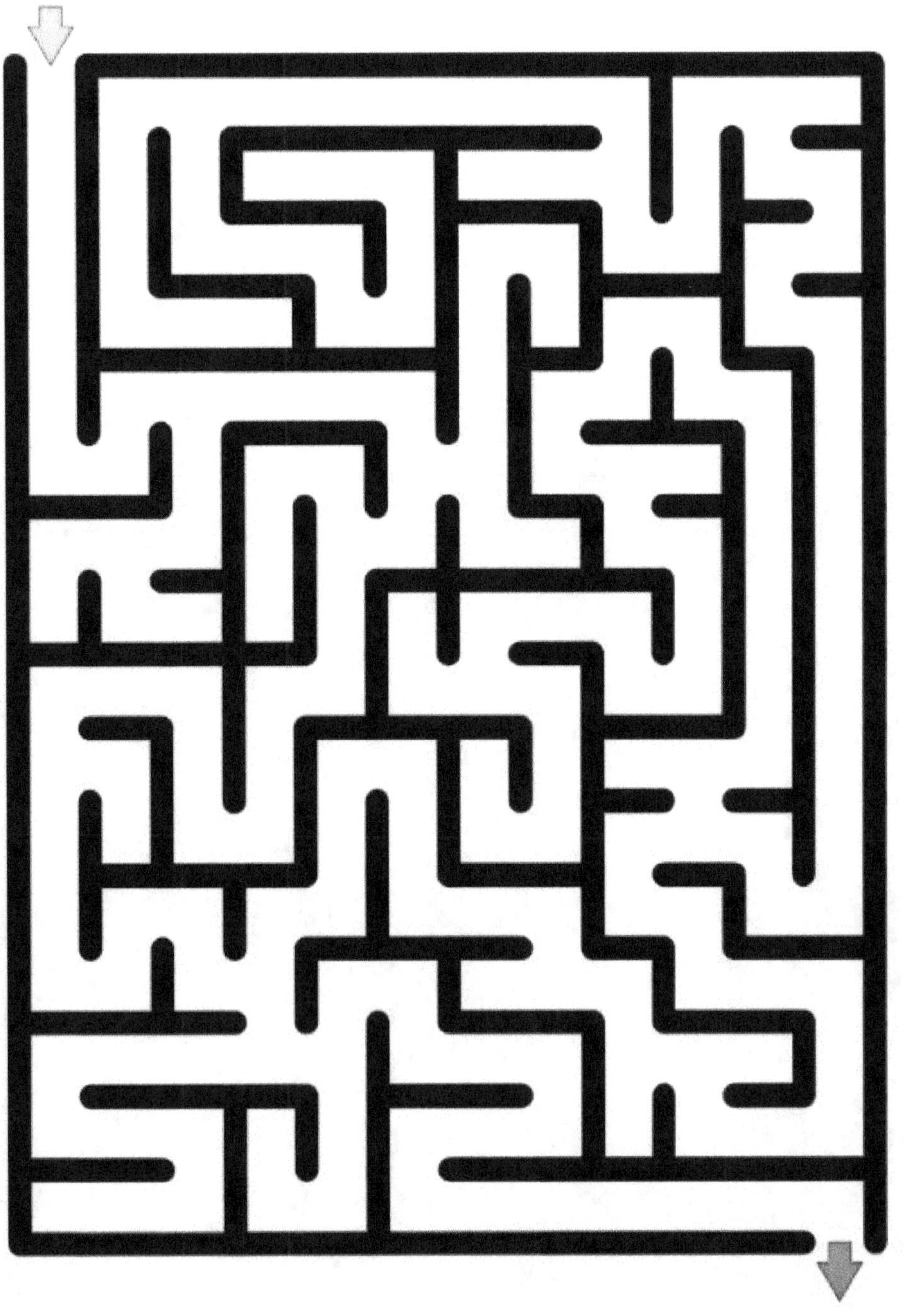

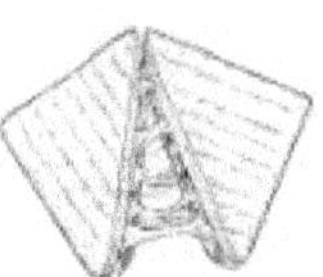

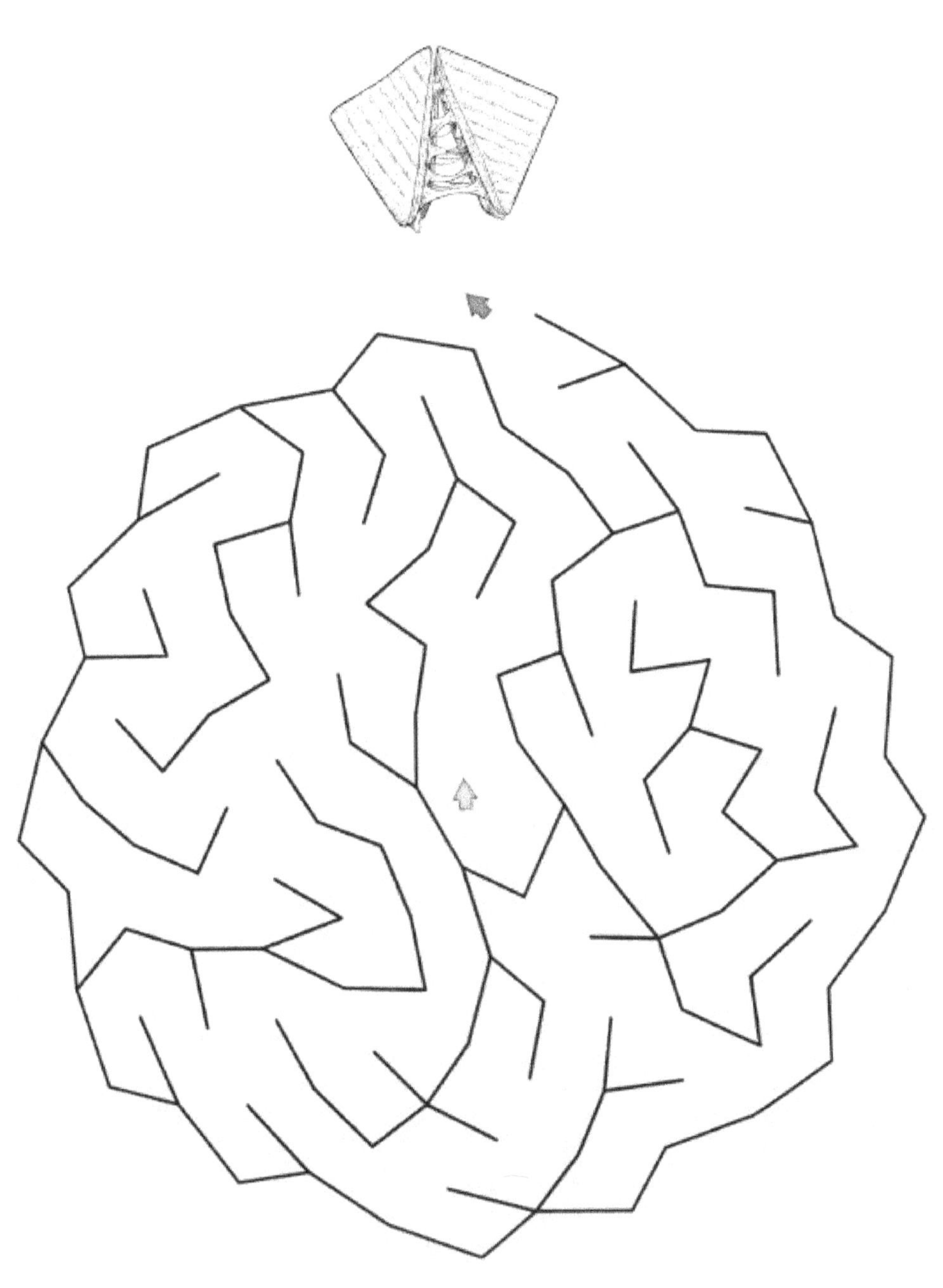

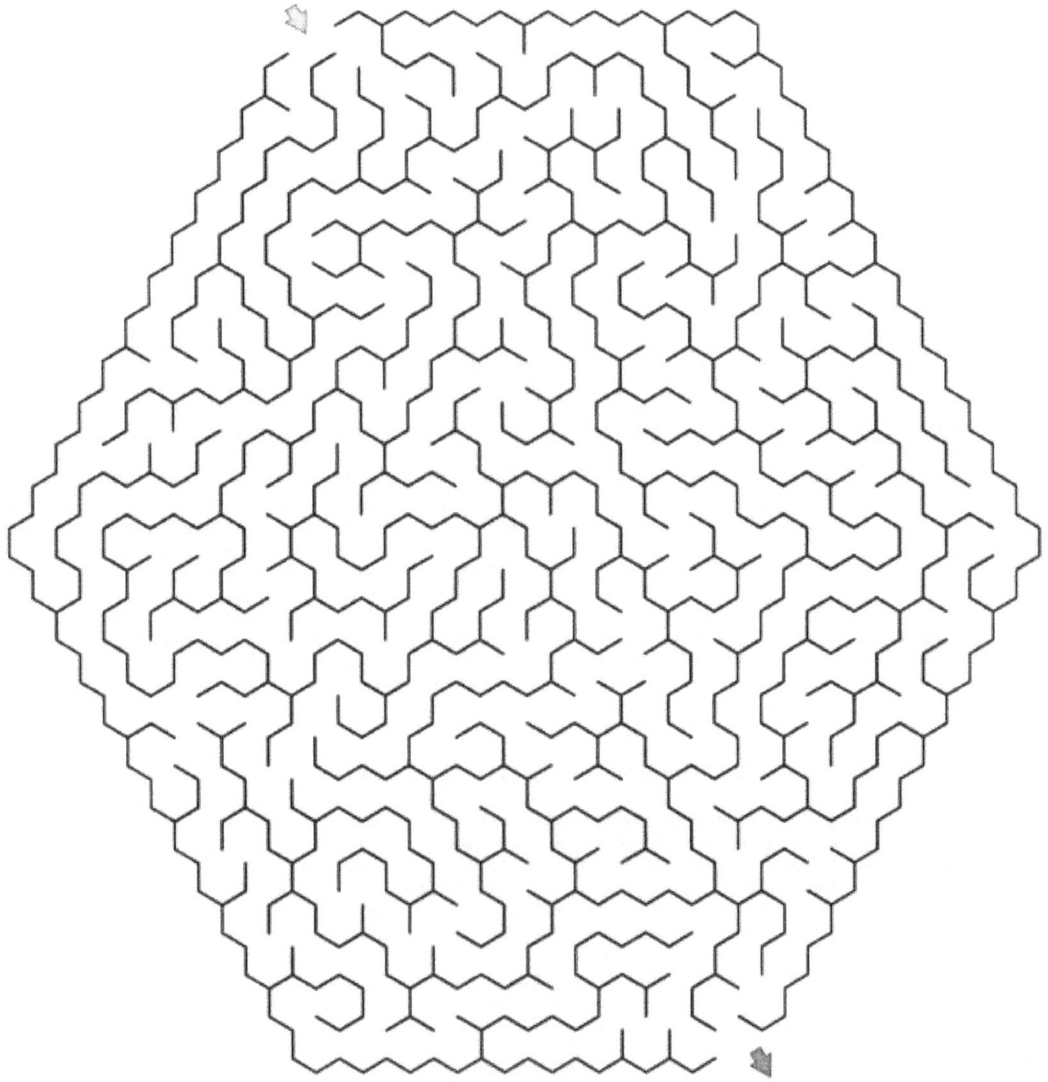

www.ingramcontent.com/pod-product-compliance
Lightning Source LLC
Chambersburg PA
CBHW081736250726
48657CB00010B/3302